Ye,
Surrealities

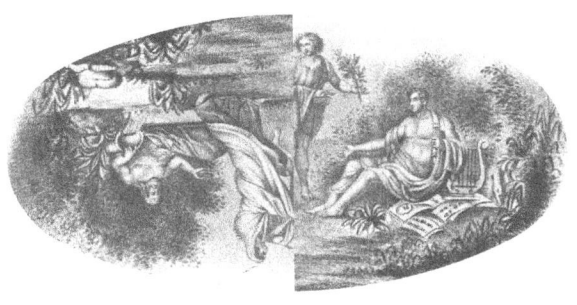

by
LA BROM

translated by
Godó Larner
MMV

YE CONTENTS
(YE BASTARDS)

*Some poems are missing from the collection and had been lost on a broken floppy diskette, having been written on a very old computer. Most cherished of these is "Swashbuckling Taxidermy," a poem about a wall-mounted deer's head which is targeted, shot, stuffed with guts and organs and then released into the forest. "The Nietzscheo" had joined the insanity of an over-philosophizing brain with it being hooked up to a 4-bit video game console that perpetually played pong....but...

INTRODUCING
LA BROM

By the Translator, 1 = 10

LA BROM, real name Lola Bromvillier, was born first of seventeen children from a cabbage patch known as Marietista Bromvillier, a five-quarters-French fat woman of intelligent and gentle fame. She was somewhere in the Paris Metropolitaine at the time according to many witnesses who would testify, leaving her without so much as an alibi to dissociate her from this master Surrealist. There were more delicate fingerprints over the ripped umbilical cord than kisses upon La Brom's forehead, wide as it was to contain many—the forehead.

There is one man that can form no such disassociation, having intimately known La Brom from his teenage years; the two would go on balloon flights across the world from west to east, sometimes purposely starving themselves as the god of voluminousness floated above the casket, soaring miles above the gentle trees, to an end that they would enjoy the Earth all the more. This friend is one acquainted with yoga and magical occultism, and his intelligence, as beseemed fit him in his initiated grade, was keen enough to translate the surreal poetry of La Brom. This man is ineluctable in this quest for the arts, ever seeking the fine compromise between surrealism and magic, between the odd and the lofty, between the second dimension and the fourth, between evasion and loveliness; and according to La Brom's own words he is also, "a seer of the sublime, peacemaker between these two factors of the undercurrent of life's turbid clitoris; a knower of great poetry." There is only one man that can understand La Brom.

Me.

I came to know La Brom as one with greater Karma than myself, and whenever and wherever I visited the surrealist circuit that went about Paris I would always make it my plan to see the Frenchmen from time to time, especially from 2004 to 2005.

To prove he had greater Karma then myself I shall explain.

.........Though my Trance of Sorrow was anything but *gung* ho—for God, too high in Heaven, cannot be said to divinely appoint the *ho*, only the *gung*—throughout the years

I was inspired by La Brom's positive attitude toward life; I proclaimed this was merely the positioning of his natal Mars ascending in Gemini, but I gathered in myself a reflective default that still ever questioned the Free Will and the bound-up destiny, the kind that stopped me having the same control over the elasticity and changeability of the elements, crying, where life for me seemed to imitate art so well that I needn't imitate *it*.

But La Brom ever dallied on the edge of his impending dooms. He struggled, I remember, financially, thinking he would win the French National Lottery simply because he "ne le perdrait pas." My "négativité" was to him a black and destructive aura and it is befitting that the only poem he truly understood of my own was "The Black Hole." This he translated into French for the magazine *Robot Débranché* as "Le Trou Noir." It is only too unfortunate that my poem of expatriation became one of *expatiation*, when the lyrics were twisted to form a diatribe on the addictions of black whores about Montparnasse. He disowned the addiction as the French literati disowned me.

So, where he would not remember to say, as I proscribed, "get thou behind me Satan," whenever and wherever I fell out of check (quite rightly as behind him was the edge of the balloon casket and a beautiful abyss), we would still quarrel over who was the headless chicken and most hopeless poet, considering the world below us was the *huître ignorante*.

In the summer of 2004 myself, La Brom and the *fillip* began a voyage in his great and marvellous balloon, the "Franc Violeur," and set upon course for Berlin via route from Paris, hopefully to find some kind of co-operation. We had planned by way of following the Belgian border a course of Luxembourg, through Limburg and into the country of that great capital—that great capital ! For what I mean by this is not that capital of Berlin, but the hill somewhere thereabouts where Count Baldwin's body is, according to La Brom, buried; Baldwin also accordingly being La Brom in a past life. If only the great crusader knew the future of his soul he may have contended with the future of his bones.

But altogether and not, bones or no bones, La Bromvillier is a great poet.

Running out of esteem upon our balloon journey by finishing several bottles of Chambertin whilst playing rook-throat chess (i.e. having to swallow our fallen pieces) we touched down in a small village which we still to this day could not name or relocate, having in our imbecility, our incredulity, our gobble-de-gookiness, our chauvinism, our sexiness, our Unidentified Flying Objectiveness,—in a word—our laziness, madness, foolhardiness, grumpiness, gracefulness, our *our*fulness, we had not bothered to look into such navigational musts.

"You got any Chambertin?" asked La Brom to the locals, in their strange sky-blue housing.

"Eh?" one replied.

"Chambertin? Have you got it?"

"Oh?"

La Brom and I rummaged through the town, knocking on doors, turning over inn-keepers and confiscating the bottles of fluid this strange *country* had on its urban mantel, until one local, speaking good French to La Brom, came up with a compromise that would see us leaving for good their little land. The plan was that this *Doctor* would hypnotize myself and La Brom, suggest us the sheep's milk was Chambertin, and let us fly away with a dozen sheep. I declined whilst La Brom, a rascally French gollyfrog, sucked on the creatures' udder like a perverted infant as we rose up again having re-embarked. As he drained each sheep, even drinking their blood, his intoxication saw him throw the poor animals overboard, landing like bombs in front of those poor townsfolk. I had no immediate objection to this as I thought the trail of sheep he left below might lead back to this rather exquisite mystery place should we lose our direction.

This is one example of La Brom. From another, printed in the French *Poeme Elementaire*:

> We as guitars lead an awful life;
> we give you all of our electricity,
> all of our shaman-sound,
>
> and we end up swung into an amplifier,
> axed into the shaman's bump-box,
> skraggled to a trash of fret-board and
>
> body, held together by a string to tease
> with your vampire teeth, stage diving me
> with you into a crowd of Ludvigites,
>
> and not thanking me or us. I demand a
>   stunt-double to be swung into the
> cymbals,
> else his head on a silver platter,
>
> held together by one string, and un-
> auctionable as the stars themselves.

—Actually this wasn't the poem I was looking for, it should have had a great climactic ending, but nevermind.

Altogether La Brom brings a unique property to the realm of surrealist poetry, as it is usually cut-and-paste annoyances that pester rather than destroy the bourgeoisie. His vision and combination of visions, paradoxes of style and perspective, and his use of language bring this jaded and clumsy darkening back to the exciting mind-game it once was. A favourite is "The Nietzscheo," where he likens the morbid, brain-squashing influence of philosophy to a video-game epilepsy [the poem is lost, so instead his poem "Vindu Siddhi"—ED]:

> Two powers thrust up against the other,
> The broth of sex and its brewing lover:
> Man's virile mystery to discover
> His undiscovered another
> And his dynamic undercover
> Quality-sepian, loosed plover
> But held semen lest his mad mother
> Matrix produce a sexy lover.
> With Vindhu Siddhi the smother
> Of my mind and not the lover
> May I produce energy mover
> To fire my songs against the other:
> That sex-broth of wankers-bother,
> Masturbatory beneath the cover
> Your super-slouch relief huffer
> And expand the speaker's woffer
> For seventy-two hours and over

And not ejaculate the flother-
Phantasm but rhyme the word "over"
Fifty two more times—and over.

A short time afterwards Le Brom had
translated one of my own French blank verse
intense-poems quite well into English, called
"Dragon Blanc":

Who says my lines are childish, lead on?
  Let him ask if intelligence hath
A word for which my mind is bled on,
  Giving its all, most seeping math,
  That is the conscience' hidden bath.
So I glare
For everyone to everywhere.

And with my voodoo spirit's orb
  I see you, thing, desired by me,
In mirrors of eyes' glossy daub;
  Touch my dream and God will thee,
  Just this be a neurotic's decree.
So teach I:
Such red be dragon, such red his eye.

I look on through rain droplets and
    bubbles
  Of windows where the nigh-time's
    higher,
Like night sea at play, my images doubles

9

Reflecting like a dream's desire.
O water-blurred man ! soul-flame fire !
Him teach I:
Such red be dragon, such red his eye.

And in his *Manifest du Beyondisme* which I have translated ahead, he justifies all:—

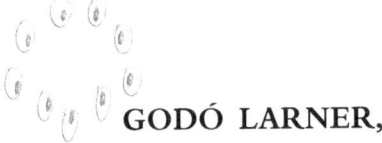 GODÓ LARNER,

England, the year 5108 of ignorance.

MANIFESTO BEYONDISM
OF

α

THE TIME is now: whatever new thing happens to be created from here on henceforth, it is only a misconception of what I proclaim to the world, **beyondism**. What is **beyondism**? Whatever it is it has no question mark stuck in its side like a thorn but as it eternally springs into existence it answers its own question, like a dragon chasing its own tail and ending up with its semen-eggs in its mouth and not saying YEA or NAY.

beyondism is the future—more than the future, it is the present of the past and the past of the future, ever quintessential and immaculately conceiving itself in the richest manger and the poorest incubator, invisibly feeding her EYE all she need, leaving scientists to BE, whilst it is the YONDER of the one thing that can cure all disease and prejudice, all philosophical axioms, of the world.

It is not Existentialism, Phenomenological Socialism, Pantopragmatism, Instrumentalism, Operationalism, Copenhagenism, Transactional Psychism; it is *beyond* 11 It is Beyond even itself, hard to catch, infinite, ism beyond isms,

ism

ismism

ismismism,

ismismismism,

ismismismismism

. . . . *ad laudanum*

β

Your new *ism* is immediately taken over by the *beyond* like a virus that spreads, but a loveable virus, a "good news."

Harvey Somebody said: "Traditional Surrealism is an Historical Abstraction while Contemporary Surrealism is Historical Surrealism by Progressive Surrealists."

Where there is progression there is something **beyond**, it is **beyondism**. It has more dimensions than the traditional and contemporary Surrealism. It is so far **beyond** the automatic sick-note that it manually crawls to lick the light-year trail of the **beyond**. The prickly jigsaw poems that *explain* surreal things but are not *surreal* are not **beyond** their own reality.

"Surreal" is short for *Superreal.* Superreal is short for—or short of—the **beyond**, which is long for "Be Yonder."

γ

Imagine a magic diamond of eighteen-hundred odd facets, dimensions colliding, edges of each fading to produce one magic globule, the colourful eight-hundreds spilling over into each other, becoming a pearl of spectral pricelessness,—can you? For mind - **beyond** - no pearl / Mind + pearl - **beyond.**

δ

beyond and its *ism*, like the Tao and its Teh, are so subtle that they are translated by many scholars into Chinese five-hundred years from now, as a kind of owing for the wisdom of the East, such that we owe them. I would go so far to say that I, La Brom ["0 - 0"— Ed.], am a reincarnation of Laocius; I am the **beyond** and the exemptus of his old life. For TAO is the old god IAO mis-spelt so that the serpent of the cross has shed its skin and become a dove. As all wise men who transcend politics and art, their devilish wisdom is pardonable by its being **beyond** the law, as Godo in his formula HVA. Therefore, to reclaim, this manifesto is: the Tao of La Brom.

ε

When I am walking my dog and it breaks off its lead, running away, never to be seen, I say "my dog has gone **beyond**." Then smack myself in the face and say

"No he hasn't, that would be impossible, not even I, La Brom, have gone **beyond**. Why should that dog, a mere four-legged mutt taste the **beyond** as though it were a poodle's testicle and Man after God's own image remain with the prigs. The **beyond** is **beyond** even that unseen vanishing point. I must slap myself again, and slap the dog doubly hard.

ζ

BIVND – 72 in the Cabala I am told. Are there not 72 degrees between each point of the pentagram? Each point of **beyond** the next when we move, as with the world, clockwise from element to element? I am not really asking you this, the answer is **beyond** you and me, but the answer is not itself the **beyond**.

η

When I go and see the local bands play their bratty rubbish garage music for blackists I wish more than ever I was **beyond**, but I can only be the propounder and the Logos of this **beyond** and not IT twenty-four-seven. Jesus was not God all day according to the creed, and Buddha was a Nirmānakaya, a puppet of Brâhma. Therefore I am a puppet of **beyondism**, that talks and dances and entertains the children of the arts. To do this I must knock this band from off the stage for playing music that is anti-**beyond**, forged in the shitty clay of their own forgettable drag-factors. You knock the band off of *your* local and we will be closer to the **beyond**.

θ

Art today is sniggered at by sniggerers and slated by slaters. For so long in fact that sniggerers have begun to slate and slaters snigger. Why? because it is rubbish.

The Turner Prize is full of attention-thieves like advertisers, only with nothing to sell, they are giving away the thing advertised for free: the informing of their idiocy. Tracy Emin burned her work to smoulders to try to send it to the **beyond**, but there was some controversy. The work actually burnt itself through shame.

If only artists were as clever as me as to pay heed to the wonderful **beyond**.

ι

How to apply **beyondism** to life and art? To life: when you fill your car with petrol your goal is to fill it **beyond** its limit, there will be some chaos but you are successful. The car will now drive **beyond** its destination. Every **beyond** that is superseded creates a new **beyond**. This is how we should live daily.

In art: the same. I conceive of the **beyond** which is infinite and unknowable. It is **beyond**

---

this manifesto, and **beyond** even that which is posited but does not yet exist. Do not chase it, even physicists have done this and failed, BE it. Be **beyond**. For all or nothing is **beyond***.

---

* This promise is not possible, or in all consideration, to be humanly fulfilled. Beyond this manifesto, first published outside of the present work in the French serial *Camarades, Aucun*, is the translation and nothing more [— Godó].

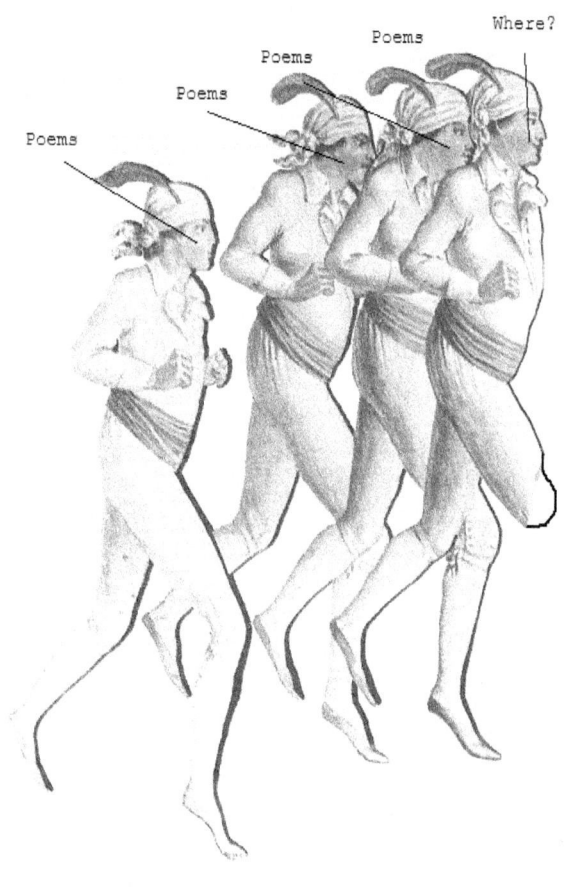

Au poèt des bruits,
le plus inspirant,

JEFF WAYNE

Je consacre ces constructions,
et couper par ceci pour
couper le ruban et entrer ma
*Métropole Merveilleuse**

---

*To the poet of sounds, most inspiringly, JEFF
WAYNE I dedicate these erections, and hereby to cut
the ribbon and enter my Marvellous Metropolis.

THE BLACK TURTLE

As the Chinese turtle-shell oracle sayeth:
"Turtles evolve from their shells to eagles
of blinding whiteness, yes?"*
The stiff-lippery of the Cabairet Voltaire†
in shiny-lead photos,
In black turtle-neck dark jousting genius
This is what I've waited for.
Who of the Voltaire will launch an eagle?
My head goes under the roll of the neck,
Into the nihlonny night of Pan.
It searches for the white.
Through the suburban pubs there.
It finds it and delivers it again to the surface
of my black turtle-neck in the one and
only form of a white unblinding face that
never found it,
And feathery never bothered evolution.

---

* Typical that La Brom should claim this passage in the *I Ching*, but I have found a more similar instance in the much-latter and much-lesser classic the *Pai Ching (Classic of Silk)*. The turtle oracle tells the legend of Emperor Yu who found the magic square on the back of a turtle that came from the river Lo. This is explained in the Lo Scroll (*Lo Shu*).

† And they were stiff. It was thought arousal was forewarned by the French woman. The track "Cabaret Voltaire" by Throbbing Gristle is a noise of pseudo-occult monkey-tumbling. Never give expensive toys and technology to apes or students "lest they turn again and rend you."

VENUS

—AND THE VAMPIRE

The Vampire [to Venus]: there is light at the
    end of the tunnel.
But to get to that light you have to enter
    the tunnel.
For this wisdom Venus put the Vampire on
    a throne.
The Vampire says it again
And Venus put the throne within a throne.
Again and again.
Throne within throne.
The Vampire [not to Venus]; now I have
with this sea of thrones an audience of kings
    to tell of the light in the funnel.
So the Vampire declared to her bowling ball
    she thought was the sphere of Venus
    as she bowled it down the tunnel into the
    light.

—DE MILO

They quiz whether Venus de Milo is better
in winter or in silk;
Better out of both, out of the mist, I came by
    inroads to the fog I cried her, armless,
My brain shouting for intelligence to depict
    this unblushing.

And there she was, at the dawn-centre of the
   fog ,
Donated tentacle arms.
She was called back to Heaven by the name
   METATRON, for which she, hugging
me, in green sloppiness of below-zero,
beside two, gave no answer in the best
tavergisation, the stare.

Now in the hug before her of coiling green
triple-helix,

In the News and everything,
Proves portable darkness.
That is: the power and expletive of her spot-
   lightning I came to enjoy in the untying,

LIVING ALONE, 1920

I live alone in a house made of bricks,
by bricks ("gather round, my numpties,
round my numpties") and sit in my
rocking chair waiting for the new world

war. The ivory of all, including the
telephone, have a dormant ineffectiveness as
the cat purrs and the pendulum flicks time
away, my rocking is unemployable and the

last crumb of sandwich and I witness the
capers of Spring-Heeled Jack, the mythical
monster man, prowling Vauxhall, ripping
girls blouses whilst laughing fire out of his

eyes, before jumping some twelve feet over
their heads. It is 1920 and I live between two
World Wars. My letters with cash in have
not arrived in asthma-America because the

Christmas temps at Royal Mail lose so many
thousands of letters and Christmas cards.
Big amounts of money lost, like the credit
slip of £55 I threw away as it were just a

receipt I scrunched, played with a little in
my distraction, and thrown away. Though a
boring life living alone I am always alert to
the two World Wars I live between, getting

closer and closer to each other. As I sit here
rocking I know one day they will catch up to
each other, on either side of me who live
between them; they'll crush me to a bloody
pulp, and bring me shoulder-to-shoulder

with Spring-Heeled Jack, he also living
between these Wars, to an end that I can see
him with my own eyes, maybe jumping over
one War or the other, and leaving me all

alone to die between them.

THE TICKLISH STAR

"...... and. ..... "
—TROILUS AND CRESSIDA, Act II, ii

Tickle tickle tickle and tickle.
Buddha tickles the ticklish star, saying:
 Tickle tickle tickle and tickle.
"Your sensation's a chimpish hindrance,
 Tickle tickle tickle and tickle.
"Your beams high-jumpable bars for gold,
 Tickle tickle tickle and tickle.
"Your ribby ego a sorrowing pulp,
 Tickle tickle tickle and tickle.
"Your laughter a small-eared Yankovich.
 Tickle tickle tickle and tickle.
"Have you met my four sisters
 Tickle tickle tickle and tickle?
"I see you see and hear me not I hear,
 Tickle tickle tickle and tickle.
"Moksha your laugh and I see you
  stopped laughing when I mentioned
  my sisters."
Had the ticklish star achieved Moksha or
  did it know something the Buddha
  did not?

ABATOIR OF MIRRORS *

Odd myself and Yulia walked
Shod by the phantasm of stretch
About this veined, murdersome dorm.
A shout from the architecture
Sent the abyss crashing over
Bent heads of we bloody lovers,
Figments of imagination,
Pigments of purple light like tassels
Swoon in the breathe-breeze's chopped podge.
Moons full of the bright of minds
Serial number the peacocky
Arterial puddles since it.
She, Yulia, falls in the dash,
We run on after I lift her.
"Why won't these dead deer stop swinging?
Why must they FROGGER our scatter?"
Quizzed Yulia. But answerless
Whizzed by silence with us, corridors
Gravely trammel of it all. The
Wavely mirrors stretched her a
Short fat child, my answerful whizz
Taught it as tall "you-rang?" lurch-merchant:
"Because: as 'as' is as always as,
We pause in time its 'it'. That's it".

Came the man with the discus,
Aim and razor running after /

---

* The Spanish inquisition had stretched with the same mirrors.

Before us. His athletix would
Tore us. Bloody, bloody, bloody
Bloody, bloody swinging swung deer
Muddy buddy of the mirrors.
Those really caricatures framed.
Whose? the came-the-man pursued—that's who !

Deer upon deer swung affront and
Near the mirror into our bent ones
Running no-where, deer by deer, when
Cunning and shy-of-ovation
Curtains like water closed over
(Pertains to the Exodus high)
Him who came. Yulia chopped her
Trim head off in complaint, and it,
Witchy, gave directions for the
Stitchy needle to play the ten
Inch vinyl-wheel of her head-pram:
Clinch and clench found in the powers:
Side A—"Fool Killer"- Gene Pitney.
Side B—"Sure Know Something" - Kizz.
Side C—the music of this thing,
Into the warping of red deer
And the discus man who is—
STILL ALIVE !!

Stop.
Rewind.
Eject..

THE KEYHOLE

When the day comes he will be crows.
I'm Looking, skrying through the keyhole at
    his preparing to be, in dreamy ugly
    hunk unboomed flinching and hair
    blowing attractively—blowing the wind
    away,
The vision becomes.
The aliens told him to do it, to kill the
children in the playschool.
Jesus told him to do it but he

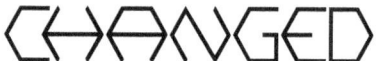

            his mind.
But not to wear the giant fish-bowl space
helmet upon his head that moves with
    the thunder-nerves of birds. Is dances.
His own idea.
Mine: my kneel is prayer.
Maybe his hand and devil-grovel will
fiercely crash through the door and my
stomach to get to my spine: Answered
    prayer.
His x-filed books say: *think of the children*,
How can I not? Looking through the
    keyhole at him before my very eye, very
    funny eye, his plans to walk to the school

like the children in the Sun with sibilant
retina; his splats of slashing; readying
walkabout like a thing of ageing stare;
His dashing and polite footsteps and grizzles
close to the screams of what will happen.
Dashing children's hair awaits—
Wait ! He is coming to the door !
The key he advances into the keyhole.
Into my very eye.
Turning it he gives ignition to the engine in
me, the one that roars *I can do nothing.*

MOST ABSURD PLACE TO HAVE SPONTAINEOUS HUMAN COMBUSTION, no. 21 and 22

(21) Paying your fair on a bus.
(22) More than two yards from Dizzy Rascal

31

STARSTRUCK
MOTHERFUCKER FROM HELL

I am a star-struck mother fucker from Hell. I'll tell you why, you who have Sigourney Weaver's economy-class mouth, with cheek pouches for a blow-job's bollocks. I, like Ricardo Ramirez (that cunt), am burning in Hell, reaching out of the flames with fingers that prop up my sun-glasses, and tweedling dance-turns that make by flairs give off sound, indestructible, lanky, dance-lurch. Neck sweating all over my *claves rectro.*

I reach up Mallet of the year out of these flames of Hell toward whom I thought was one I could lynch into the fop fop fop of my Ramirez Satanuary. But as this one turned round, this fine one on the edge of Earth, turning to see what fuckre had reached for him out of Hell (myself), it turned out to be Bruce Glover from James Bond, the father of Crispin Glover. He smiled at me, his jester face smirking, futuristic, and between his knees and crack an egg-timer that trickled sand away that meant nothing to an eternity.

I didn't wonder how he turned the timer round with his bum-cheeks. I was a star-struck mother fucker and his flashing brilliance and his still being on the Earth with time to earn Heaven pushed me back down into Hell where I dreamed of his jester-like, not-yet-malleted face.

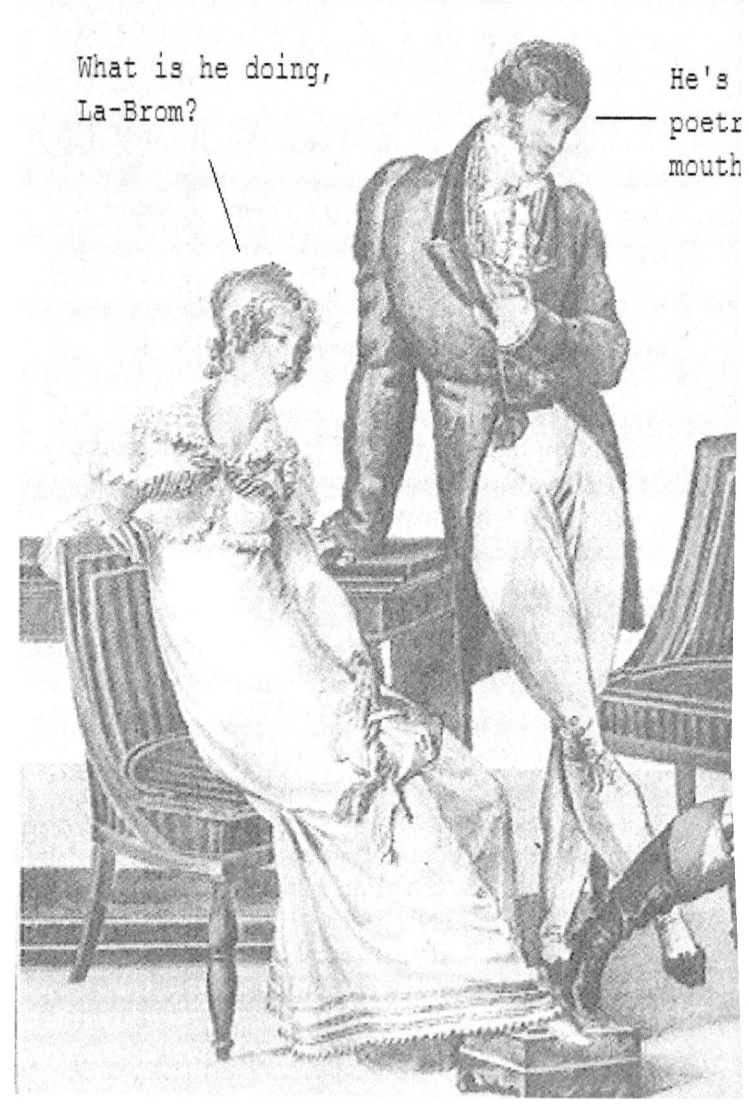

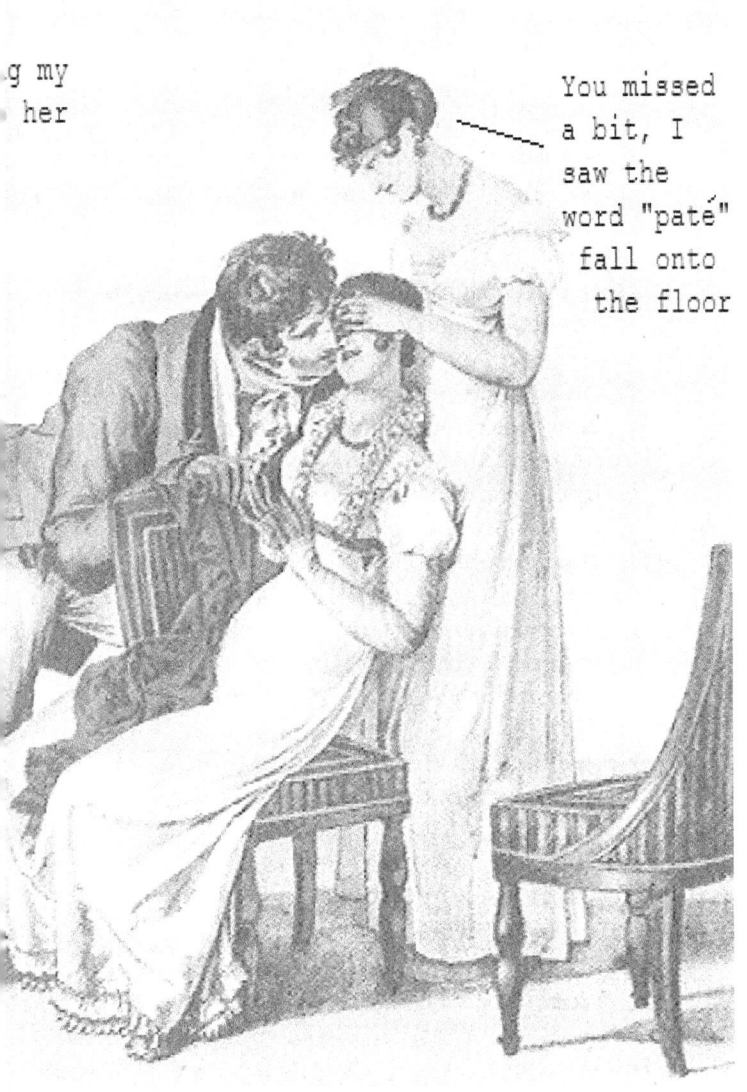

THE ACE OF PUPILS

I. Anaemic Painting

I remember when a sack washed up on
    the dirty-docks about the length of a
    body,
Washed up with Fairy Liquid bottles,
Bound like the string crown of a turkey
    breast, attracting the nosiness of
    dogs;
Distracting grey clouds of too-tall chimneys
    that launched beyond the most-giant
boring puddle I e'er kin' saw.
I somehow don't want to explain the
    repulsion, the spent simile, of
    the suspect.
Maybe I will ugly my *song-a-long*,
Or sliver him to a birth, before his head
    can show, damsel-like, calling wordless
    through the sand-castle of mud he
    disturbed,
He conquered with insectivore god-head.
And I knew what he died for.

II. Description of the Cube

From his being, his kaleidoscopicity was
    lost in the dated black-and-white

---

* Too late.

vision of the psychic detective,
And found at lost property by a scrounge.

I myself salvaged a Cube from this probable
and historic Irish poet of backgrounds.
Its three dimensions were changeable by a

little remote-control smothered in
fingerprints made by the tapping of the
tides.

On one dimension of the Cube was the Ace
of Pupils. On another a distant constellation
of a palace espied by a man behind me with a

telescope; On another a mirror. It is
Armitage's poems again, smarming a trying
New style to the twitch in my crown,

Then dad showing me a huge spider in a
pint glass, And a timeout time-ousted
'mentary on Nelson playing in both rooms

like importance; But they are not the Cube.
And I must stop here to again hide my book
mark: A photo of a photo of a naked

nine-year-old girl, as brazenly and
momentarily divine as Geminis are yappy,
Aren't you mama.

III. Channel-Strutting

When I got home from work I had to
examine the toy, My stripped balls by
potentiation smelling like perfume, like the
breasts of Noddy's mum at work, in dreams
clocked-out into.

Aw baluddy 'el !

I switched through the three channels,
Through three dimensions.

Click.
The Ace of Pupils royal flushed,
Destroying every other card, its sleeve home
to memories of the week:

That young special brunette rocker like
Noddy's sister, of *Liber 323*, with a tall
leather-coated Indian, and jittery dance-

about shoulders. A world of magic life,
piggy-backing her chum into the end of her
appearance. She looked back at me as I

wondered from the astrological Sun-dial,
sitting on Cancer, at home, and said
something to the coated and my trump card

expanded though it were *La Monde Triomphe*. "Is that your card?" I said.
And she peered into the Sun where I tricked

it, and with a *yes*, winked or winced at
        the trickery and dreamy.

                                    Click.
The man with the telescope closes on my
shoulder blade, says: "It's a hotel."
He fashions the stars, each into a step, to

ascend the higher floor of the palace which
is no longer there, disturbing the residents as
his seeing rod drags on the creakables,

though now it be they sleep forever.

                                    Click.
Through the mirror I can see he has arrived.
That I have arrived.

That we are one.   *That we are one.*

And all is one without opposition.
That three and four are one without mirror.
I remember in the eighties sitting in my

pram in the hallway, waiting for the pusher.
She and I one, I pushed it myself into the
mirror, smashing it, cutting finger-deep into

my heart, with blood clustering, gathering
about its sink. It was the fragment of mirror
where the finger-nails reflected that cut me.

The fragment of the eye reflected that was
sharpest of all.

                                    Click.
With your two of pupils looking over this
line and my Ace we can, with the triclops,
score a *Belgian House*,

Just lend me your eyes, those windows
Of soul / opportunity and save me,
And understand that using a voodoo charm

bangle on someone is so hard because you
can easily fall flat on your face, that was
lying under you, instead of around on their

enchained and dawnless reality, (Will she,
nil she?) And that the spirit in the gem can
turn any girl into your most retentive

fantasy; A woman on Fleet Street—not a
faceless Hitchcoquette in a poem but the
lady last, into a comma-soaked phrase in

phase, G-String you have to look at: but then
the clouds of instant memory; It works !!!
Understand this and I'll take care of the

triclops.

Click

Doesn't mankind cry at having to work like
a slave all his life? Am I the only one who,
without incapacity allowance, dying in a

warehouse as a neurotic, as a child in a
chimney, incarcerated? "Ah there you are"
says the man with the telescope, putting it
aside now, finding me as he did in the dark
kitchen at night, about to cut my wrists,
"I'll publish your books and everything

will be OK, and you can earn enough
money to travel, meditate, and write freely,
and not after eight-hours mind-wiping

die with that frown on your stupid face."
"The only thing I liked about those eight
hours was the young redhead Sam Young

taking notes at my absence-hearing,
Her grey polo-neck, Her clear eyes,
Her finger nails at the pen top,

Her bratty neck, her mouth massaging mine
in the naked trap of her bed."
"Yours." "Can I borrow your telescope?—

there is one uncharted star I mean to patent.
With a kiss."

Click

Scooper-pooper

Click

Salem's lot—finito !

Click

"Eat my brainy balls !"

Click
Click
Click
Click

IV. Digress

The Cube exploded and I covered the ears
    of my eye
Lest I make it onto Top of the Pops
With Franky's gay-devils,
And all three dimensions were shoved
    back in the death-pocket,
The fourth whirling:
Any new president is a shit president.
And don't pretend that you weren't
    magnetized by him.
When there is one dimension left you have
    to ask yourself if its worth
    creating,
But then you might answer,
And we'll be here all second,
On this ferry from Calais to your living
room.   O fuck off !

JANUS SIDE-OUT SYMMETRICIDE MUTILATED AND DOUBLE-BONGING THE URN OF THE DREAM-CIRCEAN

Janus side o
mutilated and
urn of the dream-
symmetricide mutila
the urn of the dream-c
metricide mutilated and
the dream-circean janus
mutilated and double
ream-circean janus side-
ed and double-bonging t
n janus side-out symmetrici
bonging the urn of the d
out symmetricide mutila
he urn of the dream-cir
etricide mutilated and
of the dream-circean
ricide mut
ouble-bon

ut symmetricide
double-bonging the
circean janus side-out
ted and double-bonging
ircean janus side-out sym
double-bonging the urn of
side-out symmetricide
-bonging the urn of the d
out symmetricide mutilat
he urn of the dream- circea
de mutilated and double-
ream -circean janus side-
ted and double-bonging t
cean janus side-out sym m
double-bonging the urn
janus side-out sym met
tilated and d
ging the urn

of the dream-circean janus side-out symmetricide mutilated
and double-bonging the urn of the dream-circean janus side-
out symmetricide mutilated and double-bonging the urn of
the dream-circean janus side-out symmetricide mutilated and
double-bonging the urn of the dream-circean janus side-out
symmetricide mutilated and double-bonging the urn of the
dream-circean janus side-out symmetricide mutilated and dou

THE METEOR MAN

It's night here in the suburbs of the scrote-map. The balls of the army ants are jangling as they Disnoid themselves through the fart wagons.

O. J. Simpson[*].

He slams his face up against the window of the house, tiny gloves on each hand and a really big machete poking out of his forehead gorehead.

He climbs into the house (so I'm told) and turns down the heating (so I'm cold), sees his wife asleep and, seeing his wife asleep, seeing it, smelling it, he reels his head back then cuckoo's it forward in marvel superpower and head butts downwards, stabbing the machete into her invisible face. She wakes rudely and remarries O.J. at a special wedding (so I'm informed) where his forehead knife is as proud as a gun loaded with lust (so I'm warmed).

---

[*] Apparently it was told how O. J. Simpson was planning to murder Leslie Nielson on the set of *Naked Gun 33 1/3*. Leslie, up on the plans of the "footballer" had halted the attack by simply punching him in the face with the end of his magnum. He then turned the gun around in his hand, holding it by the barrel, and, using the handle as a kind of hammer, hit O. J. over the bridge of the nose. All be this, the first hit was enough to actually break the nose, the second was to stop it smelling justice. Alas the weapon kept all of its six-bullets in place

THE PARADE OF TIRESIAS

I

Go forth my songs and crash head on
    into Ezra Pound's,
Reach through to the oracle your
Praiseworthiness, the god Tiresias—
For his word awaits you shining like gold
In a font of dark pink, holding up the
Firmament of each planet whence he
    sent Ezra's songs,
Beyond.

II

Go yet forth my songs and bash into
Tiresias, should his blindness lead the parade
Through an unsurrendered demolishing,
From whence Artemis' naked breasts blindly
Blinded him, giving inward, awkward
    vision.
But with real sound.

III

Go forth my songs and dive into the pool
Of Artemis; see her naked breasts
underwater, out-corralling the coral plane,
Flumpy fauna, and see no more your critics,

but remain in your body of the sighting of
magic, and only hear my order.

THE THATCHER

"Why are Five-Star so fucking shit ?"
                    —ANON

Maggy Thatcher sits shitting the bog
Her Friday meal's sundry wopper log.
Wopper wopper bip bop bip.
Her hips don't touch the rim. No hip.
She supports herself up, lifted, by palms
   Pressed on the edge of the toilet seat,
Wincing her face, scrunched, alarms
   All squealing, hov'ring to entreat
Her face goes red as pulsing sighs
Foorrrrrce the shit to blast skew-wise
Into the bog of Maggy's party,
Fiddling her stocking toes so darty.
What? Was that a sob I heard, Maggy?
   Think of England you grannifrost witch,
Its balls "tea-bagging" handbag baggy
   And it Thornchers Falkland boom-ba-
      bitch.
You bitch you ! she shittittittts some
   Gruesomely-taxed Ethiope* ploppits

---

* It was suggested by La Brom that, rather than send food to the third world countries, we should send fly-spray. He sent this proposal to the Red-Nose Relief Fund, as well as donating some 1,000 + Euros (£800) on his stay in England, and, naturally, he met reply in the most disdained voice. The actual reply from Benny Harrelson was "do you know what fly-spray in the face can do to man, woman or child, especially with malnutrition?", "yes," replied La Brom, "but I wasn't necessarily indicating that it should be sprayed in the face. No, it should be sprayed on the food we send them, the *fly-swatter* is saved for the face." The

In cries of relief from her shittitt bum
  That did not no never quite stop it's
Talking into the nineteen eighties.
One spasm kicks her leg the (maties*)
Handbag aside, emptied to bits,
  Her gritting teeth through pouted mouth-
sides
Foams bubbles out of the gums it grits
  In super-agony that collides
Embarrassment with e'er so gruelling
Strenuousity and red-faced fuelling
And finally the spool of bear shit
Like a rip-cord slizzers down, swear it
Made her speak in Thatcherist relief
  Where the red goes down for her wheezed-
out
De-shitted granny build's disbelief
  Face in a sweat now that her knees doubt
There will be more clapping crap to zap
When the deep splash deserves a nap.
Thatcher's head tucks through down her lap
To swear at and bite the shit stalactite—
The filthy cunt !†—Brazil carrot in bite.

---

conversation and correspondence went nowhere, and Benny
continued his fly-on-the face documentaries.

* This word appears in the original English

† There is an amusing anecdote attached to this word. There is a
computer at the French Science Museum, very popular with the
children, that asks twenty questions (to be answered "oui" or
"non") before telling you that your chosen animal, vegetable or
mineral is this or that. If after twenty questions the computer has
not sussed the organism it will say "I do not know what this is,
please tell me" for which you are free to type in the *new* thing of
the Kingdom to be added to the computer's database. La Brom

Yes, you're right, she lifts her aaaiirrd
And grins with er big aaaiiiirrrdddd,
Seeing in lookyism the fire
Of the IRA's bomb blowing dire
Up the corridor Beyond the bog
  Boggle, a wall of fire down there,
Her allies fire-balling the clog
  (An evil dance). Fire-faces stare
Out of the firewall at her throne
  Of constant constipation, clasps
Constable Constantinople clone.
Reaching out. Reaching out undead
From the corridor's flaming dread
Her Ally only wants the Thatcher's help
So she reaches back. Invites the "help,"
Lifts her mummy ass from the toilet seat
and.........

WIPES HER FUCKING ASS WITH HIS
FUCKING COOKED JAW-BONE / HIP.
SAYING: I. R. A.?... now *you*. R. A. !

---

typed in the specific rude word after confusing the machine with
six-legged planets, and herbivorous coconuts, and that word was
none-other than *cunt*. There were of course those partakers of
the machine's quiz who ended up with the twenty-first question
is it a cunt? I've heard that the rapper Fifty-Cent upon visiting
the French Museum brought this flashing answer without it
asking any of the previous twenty questions at all.

AUTOSTRANGULAIRE

I

From the moment you clock into life the
Rubble follows you wherever you go,
Dragging your brains over the factory that
    sprinkles junk at your thinning body,
    voiceless and evil you might be.
For every hour overtime your face
    sucks in inches more, far from the men
    quite unlike this,
Whistling their cheeks suck in a little.
But secretly, like the snake in the basket,
    your thin face sucked the tunes out of
    their faces' jolly provocation.
Doing requests.

II

The rubble follows you wherever you go,
And the mezzanine and metal scaffolding
    stabs into your skin, the dental gummage
    fucking your life-force up,
So much that in approach of a pretty polish
    girl in a nightclub who was a maiden last
    weekend frowns at your petition,
    seeing the metal of your occupation
And her reflection in your skeleton,
Waiting on another corner of the bar as a

    $3.80 lying prozzy, paid in Smirnoff,
fucked in light of.
And you work for more than this?
Or less than yourself?
Again: who are you?
Are you me?

III

Before it happens all over again the exciting
    onanism,
Nanasm,
Of the half-screeched *doing* of dawn with its
    orange abounding of mint-scented light,
Your imaginary friend unlaced from
    imagination,
You'll wrap your hands around and around
that which was thought Indian by the by,
Give one last squeeze for the freedom of the
    Proletariat,
Locking Porphyria in the thumb,
And with forearms crossed over the chest
        like the most messianic your long hair
        that is painted by once-only dunked
        brush of magenta-till-dry,
You encore-hang yourself with it;
One long magenta path your spirit will
shimmy up to the Heaven.
Clocking in.
Earning light.
And the rubble, faithless, can't follow you,
my friend.

THE VENTRILOQUIST

O how Percy the playwrong loves to apply
    caravans to the speeding sneezule.
"Bless you."
"Blessed we are, Holiday Puppets."
O how he dived his sixty-four tentacles into
    the puppet's encroachable spines, each
    talking in quattrocentist dialogue, of sixty
    -four marching gossips.
The knapweed-hidden exuviae of Percy—
O how.
O how he got it all right in the show of
    sixty-four wooden alopeciacs, the choir
    of his mega but mighty slurs, researched
    in the half-moon lemon-twist on the rim
    of his depths.
O how the new religion in them burned as
    Percy-God flew over power-lines, his
    voices spreading his words through the
    neighbours,
Spreading his own power lines—verses of
    power.
I suggested we question what dangles from
his scalp, if it was indeed his whole body
    or the body of puppets, or a body of
    a puppet.
O how he didn't but I did think that the
    country of his speakers was cold in
    summer.
Four-hundred insurgents wanted warm

hands in the one warm puppet *Maria*,
All raped her with cold unbelieving hands
   at which four-hundred voices gave the
   command from Maria's wooden mouth
   like roots of lightning,
They spoke Percy's mind, broke it in half
   Even,
Just as their bolts spoke and broke Maria's
   Mouth, which said:
" I wish I was human,"
And the four-hundred hands applauded
Percy's *O How*, smashing Maria's bones
   together,
The smoggy sky in the back of this vision,
behind the flight of Percy, is making it all
   so fucking boring !
Therefore I hate humankind,
I hate Maria's mouth.

ÜBERBILD MENU

Emila | *Med kova,* | *Moznosti* |
Dialog | *a, Bilder* | *lexicon* |
By Jan Svank	Meyer -	---------
---------	*Opus II:*	*2, Quadri*
ga Part 2	*Mörderisch*	*er Amor* |,
*Samurai,*I *Lulu, Des*	*vater des*
Gedankens	*ist, Sheila*	*(Hypergog*
ia) by Pet	er S. Rab	el ------
---------	---*Nascent*	*Aphrodit*
e by Rich	ard Geno	Vese ------
----------	----*The Eye*	by Kukl-

THE MOONBEAMS

They are not just fancies of the full Moon
    these spectral faces.
Not like the stray beams of the clumsy
nucleus of the world—its own faces.
Of what matters.
I, in dreaming by the fence-side that I could
kiss the mouth of them distilled to be empty
    of politics.
Sleepwalking.
Sleepwalking the dog of indepletable cloud
    that nevertheless rained cock-legged on a
    stalk of something else.
In the invisible-winged spirit of night she
nameless ran, to be called, unnamable,
named by the moony the cloud unveiled,
Could even be barking.

My sleepwalk ran after her little tip-toe.
She let it ripple the wallowing and yellow
Moon under the lake,
Waiting for it to still I reached to kiss her
Moon face, and the dangerous alarm clock
    beside the bed screamed, tried to stop me
    from falling into the ripple of her
    salivating Moon.
To take me to the mortuary that pays.
It woke me just too late.
I fell in that lake.

WAR OF THE WHIRLS

H. G. Wells waged war on fictional London.
Orson Wells waged war on rational
    boredom.
George Pal waged war on theatrical
    condom.
Jeff Wayne waged war on those moments
    of chaos in me before a universe is
    broken in, a dictator, listening after
    listening, of musical wisdom.
HBO waged war, I think, on school
    nights. . .
Frater Opetha waged peace on *balls of shit*
    in an old man's nappy.
Donald Sutherland.
Spielberg waged Tom Cruise on the world,
    and, though deaf of war-crimes that
    terrorist-roast the cities of the heart, was
    five-star-given by medal stealers of the
    level.
Of the seven, Jeff alone conquered, implying
    the Heat Ray to the cold impotent
    twilight.
A twilight that,
If not a wolf-whistle from the uncordoned
    sprog of girl,
Then by my dead guts alerting my hazy
brain,
Its gutless corr-phwoar-thank-you-whore
    and loveless Brewster's droop, of my

millions.
My millionettes.
Only the womany rump or lower-tummy
  sitting on my guts in kilogrammatic
  kiss-of-life,
Woman weight,
Pressing, squeezing the Heat Ray of the
  svadistthana to my hazy brain can
The slingshot effect: for all the Moog
  perambulations I will in like, alien-
  mysterious, burn and conquer the burn
  of that which can smug the gut-bolts of
  wonder.
                Ulla La !

SECADES FROM LAST

You say this man with no eyes looks for
    himself in his shadow?
I will be ready if he fails,
Turning himself toward my own
That shadow-mimics a woodpecker
    on the breast of my love.
He will not find himself but the squark:
KEEP AWAY FROM HER.
Not even pecked out eyes stopped him the
    first time.

THE MINOTAUR

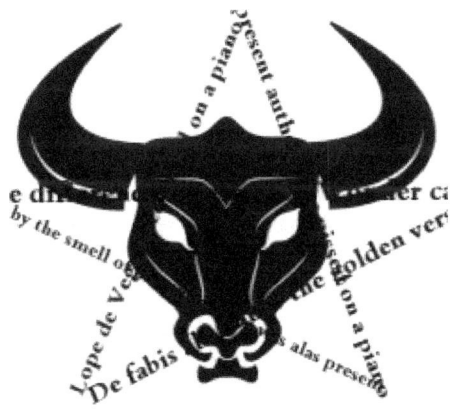

Lope de Vega once wrote a poem on a piano.
The present author once pissed on a piano.
The difference: Beethoven<>Wonder came
to deaf<>blindness *after* the former.
By the smell of piss the author is alas
   present.
"De Fabis Abstinuto" —*The Golden Verses
   of Pythagoras.*

THE FOSSIL OF NARCISSUS

The planet Mercury takes approximately, but not unstealthily, eighty-eight days to circle the Sun. This means each of the four seasons sees a complete movement of the planet, winter as summer; autumn as spring. It takes twelve hours to revolve on its axis; its day is thus 1/2 of our Earth day. It is the closest planet to the Sun and of a leaden hue. These facts were probably not unfamiliar to the Lieutenant F.X. Boschmier, though definitely unrespected. He chose it upon himself to set the course of his unpenetrated bubble of privacy about the Sun at exactly the same speed as that of Mercury's orbit, eighty-eight days to the second, lapping by seasons.

The clockwise widdershins of his space bubble on the near-exact same plane of that planet left a future collision most foreseeably slight. I speak with both the tongue of a spokesman and of an adder—because I now hiss upon his deliberate mistake. Seeing me as a *tired cunt* (unquote), uninspired writer and childishly a Rabbi Williamite, he *chucked da'an*, to put it in context befitting his clumsiness, a meteorite wrapped in some sort of paper. I could hear this weapon smash through the window of my quarters; my eyes at that time beset through the telescope, looking far, far to his face; with but tens of moments to remain intact, it leered victoriously at me through its black circular frame. I bent to pick up the meteorite—it was burning hot—and I quickly unwrapped the piping letter to find the following epic, written in the meter of Hopkin's *The Wreck of the Deutschland.*   I looked back through the lens to see—nothing. He was gone. And this was his last living strategy against the god which dwelt in the other sphere; the smarter god who reigned ingeniously in the other sphere.

Narcissus great !
He slept like a matrix
In the doorway late till eight
As his dominatrix
Wife lifted, waved the child's hand goodbye,
Adieu, adieu to his mind drooping
animatronics,
Filching in the lava-lapping by.
The door slammed like Hell's unbendable gate.

THE END

—who knows?
An end implies a means,
As a bottom supplies pose,
Applies salamandrines
To the dappled-in-desire ring-wench.
The BEGINNING was Narcissus and a picked
rose she preens,
That, like himself, for a sweet stench
Decapitated for her flat cute nose.

Must you dangle

Your brain in the Heavens,
As bate of a monstrous angle
Or quadrant, three sevens
Flicked in its leviathan eyes, to storm?
Storm it a prize of unscaled pro-bound bones
from
Devon's Green and grown land? O You
must? You worm !
Then prize your fangs fox, O beast, O bangle.

Like a new Gogh
Turning up, turning up,
Oil-rigged rug to-and-throw
Give me for silver sup.
Give me all nonsense on the go.
Give me Hurricane Penny as she look
On the graphic map, as a swirling white lily-
legion, pup
Or who knows what magic-flannel fluke
Will melt your flesh, trickle, treacle, taco.

If Narcissus
Could converse with the birds,
Like the gold marquis us
Parisians window-glimpse, whirlwind
girds
The song of golden Parisian sky,
He'd hear their were-warbled strain sere its
lyrical blood-curds,
And not least Blake's water-spiritry
That tilted his brain, poured vision its "piss us."

Damocles sword !

(Alias the sharp mind)
I call you through the ford
    Of Lava to hazard his dumped kind,
Swing over his head and report all
Of his diagonal-in-bitter-insanity mind,
    Picture the paracetamol
Fail his burning barking boiling horde.

        Has he phoned work
        To declare his illness?
    To declare eyeballs lurk
        Over the dawn's seeming stillness?
    The quilt of lava need not quiz
    His sleep in that, the next day at work, being
                *what-thou-will*ness
        Will give him a guiltiness, viz:
Blacken his spirit by the system's smirk.

        [Narcissus, one
        Feels like you as these lines,
    This meter Hopkins
        Only can master stiffens spines,
    Brings me back to an ascetic heart
    Attack shooting down the left side that I fly
            to God's right. Wines
        Of blank verse may drunken the swart,
But the meter is the sober cun—]

        "Yark, Yark you git !!"
        I hear Narcissus scream,
    Scream at his image lit
        On the lava like a fire's dream.
    At last Zeus in Heaven tilts the planet

So all the ocean of molten, burning, searing
lava-cream
Runs, paper-destroying the gannet
Of pretty Narcissus, sparks for spit:

"AAArrrrrghh
Aaaarrghhhhhh
Aaaarrrrrghhhh
Aaaarrrgghhh
Aaaaaaaaaaaarrrrrrrrrrrrggggggggh
Aaaaaaaaaaaaarrrrrrrrrrrrggggggggggghhhhh
Hhhhhhh
Aaaaaaaaaaarrrrrrrrrrrrggggggggghhhh
Aaaaaaaaaaaaaaaaarrrrrrrrrrrrgggggghhhhhhhh !!"

SONNET:
ON ROYKSOPP'S EPLE

On the night I heard the dissonance
   Of track [2], the night dissonance chimes,
   And tiny strange twinkles that mimes,
It seems, the wordlessness / resonance
Of brain storms like cuff-link accidents
   Pricking the veins where love's blood
                      swims,
   I could feel sex, rearing paradigms
Of sensuous to-the-touch cadence:
   Disco lights of R∂volution bar,
   A dishy brunette Julie Styles,
   Page-three girl Jo Lawden are
   Some of the babes I leant the wiles.
They remind, like ships in neon-night,
That track [1], before, is love before light.[1]

---

1 The first track *Easy* was the hit of the time. It played at the
seaside when I crossed a magical girl twice on two different
occasions, in two different spots. Everybody sung the lyrics
(taken from Bobbie Vinton's *Blue on Blue*) as "who are you?"
Given this occasion I wouldn't else opt.

RODIN STREET

"Say the word, that at thy command my
    angry god may have mercy,
And that my goddess, who is wroth, may
    turn again,
The darkness hath settled down, so let
    my brazier be bright."
        —NERGAL BELATSU IKBI,
            Iniminima Suilla, ll. 85-87

It is that time,
For Auguste Rodin to walk down the
    street of the future,
View all the mannequins in the windows,
And think to himself that commerce has
    mass-produced the sculpture
And that it could be said of him he is
    the scalpel pointing at the eye
    of M. P. whosoever.

It is that time.
Rodin contemptuously, spermatically,
    maybe scrolling his paper up
    to twat the stone-commuters,
Highlighting on an escalator like that of
    the showroom,
The window inbetween Rodin and his penis-
    housed town,
Feeling very perfused,
Clouds on unseen conveyor belt said to look
    like characters of a lesser zodiac

of a greater, still unseen, scalpel.
"This isn't my town," says Rodin
"Rodin snipping a toe-finger
"Rodin, one, changing a bulb
"Rodin sinking a ship
"Rodin twatting a Warhol
"Rodin giving wrong directions to a
            dolphin
"Rodin trailing a blew pantaloon
"Rodins sending birthday invitations
"Rodin dialing a long long number
"Rodin by a toaster
"Rodin showing leg
"Rodin slow motion smoking
"Rodin suggesting Belgian chocolate source
                        of the sickness
"Rodin not caring if you like him or not
"Rodin the fifth Flock of Seagulls."

Was it not the shop windows like prison
visiting panels that shook you?
Nor the stained glass that veiled your souls
in colours of the story of an Absinthe-
dimmed Genesis?

Your flame-thrown tardy tank-madrigal
fodder, Your reversed film showing stone
crumbs flying to Warhol's head and
shoulders, forming a slab, where your chisel
flinches back with laughs,

Your unpadded cell;
These are your shining powers, Auguste

Rodin, And, well it is believed that you *had*
had mannequins too in your day, my ploy is

unbought by Hollywood,
The last thing in the shop,

Like Balzac's bust with an on-sale tie where's
    knot you push up,
To crush the stone head of him who would
wear it, and only *it* lasts in your hands.
An excellent Christmas gift:
The tie, the crushing *and* the lasting.

WARNING
Why must we die?

SECRETS

I have to confess that when I said
To certain persons that during the full
Moon I change into a werewolf, I was
Lying, during the lie I changed into

Anything but, not even a parenthesis.
I am so weak and lightless as to
Light the taper of that cannon-ball
With my withdrawal. You fluttered

In pretending to be like me, dying
Your hair dark like mine, putting
On the breaks of your juggernaughty-
But-nice charm, but too late you gutted

The gutless life in me, as I hallowed
The Holy dirty milk of you, your skin,
In the sketchbook of this mad old mind.
In fact you were too early, and it would

Never really be known if I could have
Halted the comet of your strangely
Promiscuous virginity with the
Strangely of my kiss. It wanted intimacy,

The TAO. I got it, all right !—a blender
Head that mashes my skull, the same
That sharpens out of my blind face,
Because I am the walking defeat of

Your love, from the crime walking.
I didn't know that when you walked
Around me in that dream come true,
In circles like the breasts of you, that

You wanted me to take your circles.
I was too young, stupid, but you were
Younger, wanting to be as stupid, as dark.
My emotions now just things to be

Remembered, when I listen to the flutes on
"Woman in Chains," that rhyme with
The dirty breast milk of your maybe Holy
Skin, I still wish I clothed your shoulders;

Then today that other girl in the photo
That looks like you, naked back with
Pig-tails splitting the nugget hair on the
Back of the head to unsanction the naked

Neck that breaks not the bronze from the
bottom. O the secrets of Vindu Siddhi,
To hold the semen from the pages of that
Sketchbook, and have magical power to

Unsanction the nape in the pages of life
Less liable to stick, of a lover's Bible, and
Prove to adore you is to love you.
I only wanted to take you away, far away,

I had my chest in mind.
But such a little boy I still am, you a lady,
Car-driving, child-baring, cock-sucking

Woman whom a million listenings

Of Jeff Wayne's masterpiece couldn't
Master, master peace. And I, still your
Mother-in-law's boy, with the greatest
Surreality, that I would let you disturb

My Trance of Sorrow, but instead you
Began it. The pigtail portal to your neck will
end it. Hold still.

THE
FURNISHING PEACOCK
For Vicky.

"Don't 'For Vicky' me, like Satan I never
    knew you."

Nevertheless, Vicky, like Santa, in a parallel
universe you were the one flying out of me
into the bent mirror, where also wobbled
the ladder of some Angels bleating up and
down in my climb to you—

You that had won me with a hand stroking
brunette hair behind your ear, and my own
hair behind your big Disney eyes in maiden
throb; whereof I am such a fucker to let your
love simmer away;

A perfect category of my genes simmer
away, as I was mourning over Noddy who
too is dead. This was it, that you'd pull

a book out of a shelf in your shop to a secret
portal, conker as conker splitting, and I'd
follow you into that cave, which is after all
my head, a stuffed peacock fire rug and:

Green plume-spread carpet with many
many eyes, I love You ! Here and now in my
nightmare tell me what skirts you have

looked up to splay your way, branch as
branch reaching, gusset as gusset shining,

And you can stay in me a little longer, our
house. Twenty years passed, My and Vicky's
children, scrawl of the peacock-eyed carpet,
With her Disney eyes—child and horny
sheik carpet—are meshed with the genes of

literature and ever attractively marble-
arching the days together; and when Vicky
puts on a sweater, struggling, her
giant caring tits, faceless for an hour, suck
the family's nutrition points up, in a
brunette's warm and round bouncy-castle of
slightly hyper-density.

Roll with Me Vicky of this dimension !
Roll with Me Vicky on this carpet of
peacocked Disney Eyes,
Roll with me though the carpet spread over
the walls and your face—Disney eyes as

Disney eyes roll— like the fiction of echoes
and the truth of swarms, for in this other
dimension I love you and learn of you, for
our children's sake and for God's,
Whither could this bump under the carpet

be your unprocurable bodies, O my family.
But stripped up, the chalk line on the slate,
round as round is caring, of your form, O
our Vicky, echoes your invisible body

In an ending of a nightmare involving a

whirlpool which I have changed.
I love you across this divide.

ONAN MANUELLE

Like the year her chest has two delectable
    Seasons,
Where runs like ink Persephone hiding.
The city its unmoving soarings,

And the surrealiste, movement,
Its many colourful words slammed together
annoyingly,
On black,
In auto.

Look at me fighting to set alight a new one,
Something to dream over,

When bled I am of all the semen of magic
Forever Manuel Onan and the black after
the fire. . .

As for me I want to write, though the thin
exhaust piped finesse gashes the brain cells a
nine-inch trap, Manuel and homeless

aneurysms (catatonic water),
Then so long choking my chops that my
arms have evolved into wank-levers on a

diagram, that cannot shake hands with Jadil
Toyen or one-wing straddle-fly over
Godnik's dog-rose, with still no friends and

no names to share with you. And because
liquidated imagination and the poet
have tried to reconcile in the form of a toast,
And been disallowed this where no arms
clink,

I have come to write this poem in that
semen. And in this not well—absent from
work—work- Absent—spent—the last line.

OTHER BOOKS AVAILABLE
BY

GODÓ LARNER

NIGHTMARES TO REMEMBER ME BY
(as "Charles Wong")

555

THE BOOK OF OTIOSE

TALES OF MAN IN FILM FANTASY, no. 1

MUZZALMAN IN HELL
(as "Kenichiro Hamlet")

INSPIRATRICE, AND OTHER POEMS

UMBRELLAS UP!

Z301278
(4 vols, as "Sri Dhananjaya")